The Colors of Me Without You

Liz Janis

BookLeaf Publishing

India | USA | UK

The Colors of Me Without You © 2022

Liz Janis

Presentation by *BookLeaf Publishing*

Web: www.bookleafpub.com

E-mail: info@bookleafpub.com

ISBN: 978-93-5744-969-4

First edition 2022

DEDICATION

In loving memory of my Grandma Merle, Papaw Rick, Uncle John, Great Uncle Dale, my father Robert, and my Granny Lynn. All gone far too soon but hopefully this can be a piece of you that carries on.

ACKNOWLEDGEMENT

A heartfelt thank you to my family and found family for loving me and encouraging me.

An extra thank you to Brit, Connie, Daniella, Devin, Kathy, Lily, and Stacy, who put up with me constantly second guessing myself during this process.

Gray

I can't tell if you were truly gray,
Maybe I just remember you that way?
Wondering if it was the demons you fought?
The consequences of a life you wrought?
It was too late,
To re-write all of your mistakes.
The first glimpse in my life,
Of a conclusion of years' strife,
I wonder if you had another go round,
If we could keep your feet on the ground,
Knowing what we do now
About how your demons slowed you down.
Did you know the wounds your kids carried
around?
Your haunting presence that didn't make a
sound.
I hope you know that I understand,
Sometimes life takes the things you had planned,
It throws things out of control,
Sends you down a hill where you had to roll,
All alone through a story that will go untold,
Through a life that was cold,
Through streets that felt broken,

I hope when,
If there's a time where we meet again,

You'll know that I didn't know then,
How you struggled with demons you called your
friends.

Pink

In the full bloom of spring,
Remembering me on a swing,
You were there too,
I don't hold many memories of you,
I keep the few that are clear to me,
Locked in a box of other precious memories.
The story of you through my eyes,
Never got tainted by a life of lies.
Seeing you only through childhood purity,
Maybe through me you left with the surety,
That your name carried some good with me,
That through you I knew what I wouldn't be.
In retrospect,
I can respect,
The fact that you used your time left,
Trying not to leave this world bereft,
It's something I can understand,
In the end you tried to take a stand,
Against the rused tarnish,
That ruined the varnish,
On the hall of memories,
A place full of your life stories,
Wondering if in the end you found peace,
In your passing you found release,
While I miss what could have been,
Wondering, how, why, or when,

There could've been more time,
For you to reach your brand new prime,
A flower planted on the brink,
Spring blossoms are coming in bright pink.

Charcoal

I used to think of you in tragedy,
A figure in my life that was snatched from me.
Never considering that all versions of you,
The good, the bad, and the ugly too,
Were all sides of the same rolling die,
That each side had their own lie,
Maybe that's mature clarity,
Realizing that the disparity,
That who I knew and who you were could both exist,
Even with one part hidden in the mist,
I want to pass on lessons you learned,
The wisdom you earned,
The hard way,
So that someday,
When I've achieved everything I could dream of,
I'll know it's because even in the charcoal
colored actions of your past,
You left something that would last,
Your mistakes weren't wasted on me,
That due to them life won't treat me like a flea,
I wonder if it comforts you,
That in the end you accomplished this last thing
you set out to do.

White

I remember you that night,
Knowing something wasn't right,
Waking up at two in the morning,
Heart rate in my chest soaring,
The pain was like a blinding light,
All I could see for a minute was white,
Somehow in my soul I knew,
We had just lost you,
The sense of dread that came at dawn,
With a text message saying you were truly gone,
An agony that didn't seem fair,
Leaving a space knowing you should be there,
You were someone I didn't know I would love,
I'm sure I wasn't the surprise grandchild you
dreamed of.
You were a gift that I got from a bad situation,
I showed up and you needed no explanation,
You loved me like I was always meant to
belong,
Like I was just a new verse in a song.

I could say I didn't fall apart,
But you left an imprint on my heart,
So large that your absence felt like a year
without rain,

Like the wind was so dry, breathing caused me pain.

Tan

Oral history is one of the oldest traditions,
Older than writing and religions,
You were full of stories,
Long ago memories,
Details the history books wouldn't tell,
Remembering your voice so well,
The world as you knew it,
I remember how bright your eyes would get,
Your tales of travel and exploration,
Your service to our home nation,
I could listen to you for hours,
Your words had super powers,
The world lost an orator for the ages,
One who never put pen to pages,
Wishing we'd put your stories in a book,
Filled the tanned and well worn pages of the
journeys you took,
I can only hope to tell,
Stories like yours half so well,
We lost a true piece of history,
Leaving so much time as a mystery.

Royal Blue

The sound of shuffling,
A fresh deck of cards ruffling,
The backs covered in royal blue,
Always remind me of you,
I remember learning thirty-one,
Watching the game long after I was done,
Getting nervous when you were on your honor,
So many times you were almost a goner,
You always seemed like you were having fun,
Regardless of whether or not you had won,
You were such a happy person,
No matter how your situation would worsen,
You just played to enjoy the game,
Winning was nice but for you it was all the
same,
I remember your laughter,
Even when realizing someone had the card you
were after,
When you would hand out cards that were for
me at least advantageous,
Your joy just to sit and play the game was
contagious.

Blood Red

Some nights when I think about you,
I wonder what you would do,
If the accident hadn't taken you down
Would you be happier now?
I see your memories stained blood red,
Wondering how someone could leave you for
dead,
As if there was no one who showed you love,
Who'd scream into the skies above
Wondering how to get you back?
How to put you on the right track?
They said you were gone before you knew,
What this person did to you.
I wish I could find peace in that
Yet somehow that comfort still fell flat.
You deserved a better life than this,
You deserved to live in bliss.
You were stronger than the demons that
surrounded you,
Now we'll never know what you could do.

Some nights when I think about you,
I wonder what you would do,
If the accident hadn't taken you down
Would you be happier now?

Green

I gained Celine the Mean Green Machine,
She was new to me, shiny, and clean,
While a car was no substitute for you,
She was taken from me too.
It felt like a new hole in my heart,
Another loss tearing me apart,
How could I lose this last piece of you?
What was I supposed to do?
Losing this part of the puzzle,
It was like letting my grief off of a muzzle,
It was like losing you all over again,
That car had become a dear friend,
We crossed state lines,
Got a few fines,
Traveled from city to city,
But one person's negligence destroyed her so swiftly,
Being rushed away was such a blur,
They told me I couldn't save her,
Just like I couldn't save you,
There was nothing I do could do,
Like a dam the gates holding my grief broke,
Unprepared for the emotions the accident would evoke.
I guess deep inside I knew,
I wasn't done mourning you,

Knowing you would've told me everything was okay,
That I was alive at the end of the day,
But the agony is hard to see through,
When it just shows me how much I miss you.

Orange

I know every word to Eminem's "Lose Yourself"
I was so proud of myself,
You taught me every rap you knew,
Taught me most of the curse words too,
When I got a new orange basketball
You picked me up every time I would fall,
Gave me Pokemon Cards and told me all of their
names,
Shared your love of video games,
Beat the levels I would get too scared to play,
For me there was no monster you couldn't slay,
When I was a child you were a hero that
conquered all,
So when I got older, it hurt so much to see you
fall,
Who was I to face the world alone,
When the challenges out there knocked you off
of my childhood throne?
Yet in the face of absolute disaster,
You told the world where to go and that you had
no master,
Deep down inside I always knew,
That I hoped I could be as courageous as I saw
you,
Maybe I idealized you in my imagination,

Maybe your life wasn't powered by determination,
Like I believed it to be,
But in the end you were taken from me,
I know deep down you were smart and brave,
You didn't play your life on auto-save,
But I wish you had respawned at your last checkpoint,
Instead of meeting your end point.
I hope I'm living a life where you'd be
In the background still cheering for me.

Gold

You lived your life full of zest,
Always told me you were blessed,
I know everyone called you crazy,
And while that may very well be,
You were a sun with rays of gold,
Despite the rain, your color never dulled,
I wish I could explain how much I was shocked
The news you were gone left my world rocked,
Who could fill the shoes left by you?
Who could even begin to try to?
The world lost a man with unending humor,
Crazy was such a boring description of who you
were.
How dull the world was without your bright
rays,
How quiet was the earth for days and days,
You were like a mythical creature,
Someone who wasn't a permanent feature,
But only because you weren't bound,
By the laws that keep others on the ground.

It took the ground from under my feet,
I had never considered death to be someone you
couldn't beat.

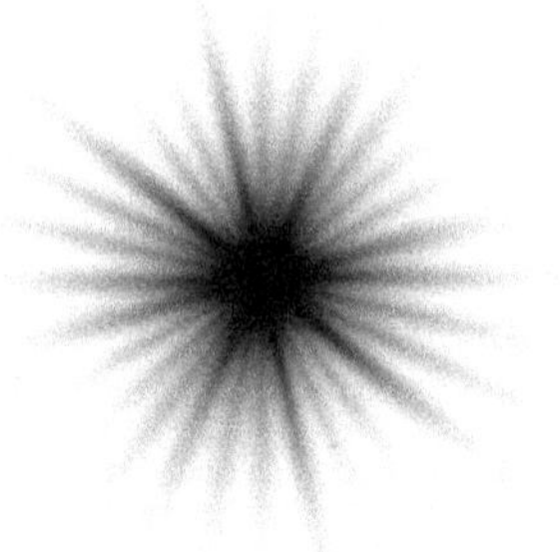

Yellow

The world without you isn't as interesting,
The pain from your loss was almost crippling,
Who else will show up in a giant chicken suit?
Looking like a hen escaped the coop?
A smoking chicken outside of a church,
All you were missing was a big bird perch.
The memories that come with missing you,
Are full of the abnormal things you'd do.
One year you were the Chiquita Banana Lady,
I laughed until I cried while others called you
crazy,
I associate you with bananas now,
I try not to laugh more than polite society would
allow,
But when I think of you,
It's the best thing I can do,
I'm left with wild memories,
Filled with worthwhile stories.
You were such an odd duck,
I'm glad that out of sheer luck,
My life included you,
You and the wild things you'd do.

Neon Pink

Neon Pink flamingos caught your eye,
You were never one to be shy,
We were sent on a covert mission,
You wanted them as a new yard addition,
Or another time where you sent us for shrubs,
Because the ones in your yard were little stubs,
This charade went unnoticed or maybe your
neighbors got a good laugh,
Four little kids crawling around on your behalf,
My cousins and I thought we were sneaky,
Looking back I think your neighbors thought we
were cute and cheeky,
Otherwise who wouldn't suspect a troupe of a
children,
Stuffing flamingos in a yard otherwise barren?
You let the boys drive me up and down the
hillsides,
We'd speed around on these joy rides,
They would jump the hills until I got sick,
To me it was such a fun trick,
It never occurred to me that you would get old,
You were such an otherworldly person to
behold,
I keep the crazy memories with me,
One day maybe I'll take up your prank spree.

Black

Never, ever did I ever dream you would go,
How could I ever be expected to know,
That somehow I would have to find,
A way to regain my peace of mind,
Somehow I can't sit with the idea that you're
gone
With how the world works and where I belong,
Please show me the stage of grief
Where my heart finds relief,
I feel like I'm being sucked into a black hole,
When do I get back the piece of my soul,
That broke off because you aren't here any more,
You held on until the bitter end,
You had a will that death almost couldn't bend,
You held on for so long,
You were always so stubborn and headstrong,
I know that I told you that it was okay,
I understood why you couldn't stay.

As much I said you could go,
There was no way to know,
How the storms inside me would grow,
I have never ever felt so low,
I hold your memories so dear,
But I'm still messed up from wishing you were
right here.

Bronze

I could tell you the family tree,
Of every 90s wrestler from WWE,
I remember all the sayings,
All the roles they were playing,
Athletes covered in bronze from head to toe,
Screaming at the TV about a low blow,
You knew all the story lines,
How all of the players intertwined,
Which championships were changing hands,
Together we were the biggest fans,
I dreamed we'd see Wrestlemania together one
day,
The universe ripped that dream away,
I'm going to take a piece of you with me,
I'll make it in person, one day we'll see,
I thought that part of my life was laid to rest,
Without you how could I cheer on the champs
we loved best?
I found new friends you would've loved,
With that same knowledge you were full of,
Having them brings a part of you back,
A part that I thought slipped through the cracks,
A piece of you that I never knew,
Would keep me closer to you,
There are you shaped holes inside my heart,
Spots I was sure would tear me apart,

But I'm lining the edges where you should be,
With people I wish you knew who love me.

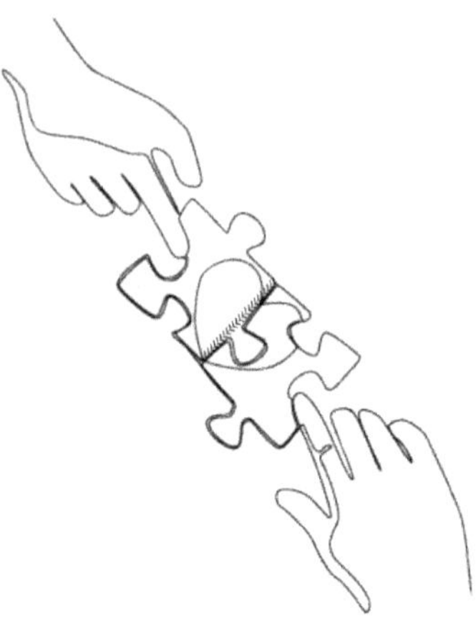

Sky Blue

I've spent my whole life wanting to make you
proud,
Wanting to see your face cheering me in a
crowd,
Losing you tore apart my soul,
Now how would I ever reach this goal?
I'm trying to live a life you would find
worthwhile,
A life that would make you smile,
I have your bracelet and now your iPod too,
Keepsakes that keep me close to you,
Even though you've gone away,
Sometimes I can hear you say,
"If you're lost look for me,
You will find a way."
Even after all of this time,
Looking for some sort of sign,
As new paths unwind,
Without you it feels like walking down these
roads blind,
Following the beat of my own drum,
But still hearing the songs you'd hum,
Clips of Nickelback, Shinedown, and Seether,
Lines from classics like Julius Caesar,
I'm taking the time to travel,
Watching new parts of the world unravel,

Before me lies a world to explore,
Knowing you wanted me to see more,
So I'll cross the globe still expecting texts from you,
A surprise text because somehow you always knew,
When I was traveling when it hadn't been mentioned,
It was like a release of any trip tension,
A simple check in,
"Hey kid where have you been?"
Going across blue skies and from sea to sea,
Becoming a person I hope you'd be proud to see.

Silver

All the old pictures I've seen,
Made you look like a star from the silver screen,
This year you'll be missing Christmas,
That feeling leaves me listless,
Silver tinsel makes me think of you,
You were the life of the party with the things
you'd do,
You kept these little light up houses and
beautiful vases,
Some out in the open and others in glass cases,
It seemed fitting someone so full of light,
Had displays that were so bright,
How does our family survive staring at your
empty space?
You were beauty, you were grace,
Everywhere you went there was almost always a
100% chance,
That you would hear a song, and get up and
dance,
You were in pain for so long,
Even though I know it's wrong,
I wish you had made it just a little farther,
So we could've made one last Christmas a little
bit larger,
I'm going to need to find the spirit of the season,

You wouldn't have wanted your passing to be the
reason,
That we didn't give each other joy and love,
You'd want us to raise each other above,
The grief of how these years have been so
rough,
I hope we can celebrate enough,
To do you justice,
Even if it's just us.

Maroon

You come to mind when I see decks of cards,
King, queen, jack of hearts,
I remember maroon poker chips,
You held the fate of a game in your fingertips,
I guess it's suffice to say,
I wish I had learned to play,
You and Dad you're both gone now,
While I could still learn how,
It feels too little too late,
I would love to rewind the date,
Ask you to teach me your ways,
How to utilize your Ace,
King, queen, jack of spades,
Now your skills are behind closed gates,
Seasons change and it's getting cold,
I wonder how long this grief storm will hold,
I still hear your echo,
How can I begin to let go?
I'm left asking why,
Looking toward the sky,
I wonder why you were taken from this place,
While my world mourns your beauty and grace.

Coffee

If I had to pick a smell,
That represented you well,
It wouldn't be hard for me,
You always smelled like fresh coffee,
The kind that starts your day,
Even when you have too many obstacles in the
way,
The smell of fresh coffee beans
Lingers even though you're nowhere to be seen,
It's even how you would start Christmas,
Before the living room turned into a big mess,
We'd all have champagne the night before,
You would dance until you couldn't anymore,
Just hearing the jukebox play Michael Jackson,
Would push you into action,
I don't know holidays exist now,
Without your joy I'm wondering how
We keep the memory of you alive,
Keep the spirit you had and let it thrive,
Christmas Eve we'll share a toast to you,
I hope we dance and sing like you would do,
In the morning even if it's just me,
I'll make sure we have fresh coffee.

Navy Blue

I remember each and every loss,
When a fresh one tears me apart it tosses
Me back out into a sea of grief,
Left lost, in anguish beyond belief,
How do I keep weathering the storm?
It feels like being here is becoming the norm,
Surrounded by a raging navy blue sea,
With rain and waves crashing around me,
When the sun does show its rays,
It leaves me in a daze,
Wondering if I'm at peace with the loss of you,
I find myself wondering what to do,
How to peel myself off of the raft,
The one I made with the pieces of you I had to
craft,
To keep me from drowning deep below,
There aren't enough words for me to let you all
know,
The depth of sadness I have from letting you go.
Whether it's been months or years since I've
been left wanting more,
I still haven't found what I'm looking for.

Purple

Hearing your names in the wind,
Seeing you when I look to the sky
Needing you to know
That I will never let you go
Losing you was never part of the equation
Wishing we had one more conversation
But knowing I can't dwell in the past
I'm keeping the parts of you that will last
Holding the pieces of you in my heart
Keeping me from falling apart.
There are you shaped holes left in me
But I'm filling them with people I wish you
could see.
I'm using your love to keep me strong
One day I'll find out where I belong.
Although grief is a restless sea
I'm starting to finally see the purple night sky
above me.

Rainbow

The world has shown me a million shades of
gray,
Taking those whom I've lost away,
But as time passes,
While emerging from the ashes,
Revising the colors of your love,
Knowing how you keep me rising above,
When the grief drags me too low,
Remembering that they say you can't have a
rainbow,
Without the rain,
If the price of loving you is knowing this pain,
I wouldn't trade this,
Not for all of the ignorant bliss,
Always feeling your marks on my heart,
But you all gave me places to start,
Lessons learned,
Scars that you earned,
Showed me the way,
Of how to move on to a new day,
I can't say I'll never feel like I'm going to drown,
But know that I will never let you down.